PAPERS FROM
HARVARD UNIVERSITY

Dear Stella Bednar,

Enjoy the Harvard Papers.

With my best Compliments

V. Antony. J. Atahavasan

8 - 29 - 99

PAPERS FROM HARVARD UNIVERSITY

Rev. Dr. V. Antony John
Alaharasan, Ph.D.

VANTAGE PRESS
New York

FIRST EDITION

Copyright © 1991 by Rev. Dr. Antony John Alaharasan, Ph.D.

Published by Vantage Press, Inc.
516 West 34th Street, New York, New York 10001

Manufactured in the United States of America
ISBN: 0-533-09366-X

Library of Congress Catalog Card No.: 90-91404

0 9 8 7 6 5 4 3 2 1

Contents

Foreword

While studying at the Weston School of Theology, I was able to encourage and help the author in choosing classes at Harvard University. I am pleased to see that he is now publishing the work he did there.

In the essay on Jainism and Manichaeism he discovered that the five ethical principles of Mani had their root (come from) in Jainism. This discovery alone is a valuable contribution to this field and good reason for publishing the paper.

Non-violence is a growing topic of interest in our times. The author gives an excellent brief treatment of this subject, comparing what Hinduism, Buddhism and Christianity have to say. The section on Hindu life is quite interesting and well done. Topics like childbirth, caste, loving devotion and image worship are given an excellent treatment. In the final part of this book the author looks into the subject of hospitality in the Bible and Kural. He compares what each book has to say on this subject.

Each of these four parts is treated with the deftness of a scholar who specializes in Eastern Religions. Each is well done and well worth the time spent on it.

Rev. James J. Fedigan, S.J.
Murray-Weigel Hall
Fordham University
Bronx, N.Y. 10458

Acknowledgments

I am very grateful to William and Anne Pelletier for their support and encouragement during my study period at Harvard University. My sincere thanks also go to Mrs. Maria Cedargren, Registrar, Harvard Divinity School, and Mrs. Linda Mitchel, the librarian at Widener Library at Harvard, who supplied me with books. Also my thanks go to Fr. James Fedigan, S.J., who was instrumental in getting me some rare books from Weston Theological College Library.

Finally I would like to thank Maria Dee and Sue Nelson, my typists, who have done a terrific job in typing my manuscripts. I also would like to thank Corinne K. Brown for her support.

Introduction

I was admitted to Harvard University Divinity School from 1988 to 1989. I was enrolled as a Minister in the Vicinity (M.I.V.).

During this period I was very fortunate to participate in two semester courses: "Mesopotamian and Iranian Religions from Alexander to Mohammed," taught by Professor Richard N. Frye, Ph.D., Aga Khan Professor of Iranian; and "A Cycle of Hindu Life" taught by Professor Mary McGee.

The first part of this book deals with "Jainism and Manichaeism—their ethics and practices." This research paper, delivered in the classroom before Professor Frye and my fellow classmates, deals with findings from Jainism, which was the ethical source for Manichaeism. Professor Frye and fellow classmates said it was the best paper on the subject and it should be published. Now my readers have the opportunity to read and enjoy it.

The second part of the book consists of four articles written for Professor Mary McGee's class on "A Cycle of Hindu Life." They are:

1. Caste in Hinduism
2. Childbirth in India
3. Image Worship or Idolatry
4. Loving Devotion (Bhagavad-Gita)

The third part of the book deals with comparative outlook on non-violence in Hinduism, Buddhism, and Christianity.

This paper was a talk given in Park Slope, Brooklyn, New York. It was arranged by the Peace and Justice Committee of St. Francis Xavier parish and the Park Slope Freeze Forum, who co-sponsored a forum called East-West Perspectives on Non-Violence on April 10, 1986.

The final chapter in this book is "The Concept of Hospitality according to Bible and Kural." This was a research paper supposed to have been submitted at the sixth International Tamil Conference on June 23, 1983, in Singapore—but, because of some unavoidable circumstances, the conference was not held. Hence this paper appears for the first time in this book.

I hope the readers will find the following articles very interesting and enriching.

PAPERS FROM
HARVARD UNIVERSITY

Part I

The author before the statue of John Harvard at
Harvard University in Cambridge, Massachusetts.

Chapter 1

Jainism and Manichaeism— Their Ethics and Practices

Mahavira and Jainism

Jainism is a monastic religion, emphasizing asceticism to its core. Its founder, very often referred to as its reformer, Vardhamana, a contemporary of Buddha, was born the son of a clan chieftain. He lived from 599-525 B.C. in Northern Bihar in India. He took up asceticism at the age of thirty and led an increasingly austere life for twelve years. In his thirteenth year of asceticism, he achieved liberation from Karma and acquired the title Mahavira, meaning "Great Hero." He is the twenty-fourth supreme teacher in a long line of "ford makers" (Tirthankaras) or makers of the river crossing.[1] The Jains, known in ancient times as Niganthas, the unattached, derive their name from a Sanskrit word "Jina," meaning "victor," or conqueror. This term is applied to the great teachers who have successfully crossed the river of transmigration. The movement Mahavira led was called "the religion of Jinas" or Jainism, the religion of conquerors. It reflects the heroic character of Mahavira's asceticism.[2] Mahavira died at Pava in the year 527 B.C. when he was in the seventy-second year of his life. "Fast unto death" was considered as a wise man's death,

3

and Mahavira fasted unto death. The title Jina or victor is applied to Vardhamana, Mahavira, the last prophet of the Jain. It is applicable also to those men and women who have conquered their lower nature and realized the highest. The name Jainism indicates predominantly the ethical character of the religion.[3] It is the only heterodox religion surviving in India today. According to the 1981 Census, the Jains form an admittedly small but nonetheless influential and comparatively prosperous community of 2,604,837 people in India.[4]

Mani (A.D. 216-274) and Manichaeism

Mani was born on April 14, A.D. 216 in Mardinu. Mani's father was Patez, a Parthian. His mother was Mariam, a Semite Christian. He was born of a princely Parthian family and spent his youth in Mesopotamia. He liked plants, trees and flowers. He heard plants speaking to him. At the beginning of his life, he was a gardener, at which time plants spoke to him and told him not to hurt them, and so he renounced working in the garden. Mani was also a physician and a well-known painter of his times. Mani always addressed himself as an apostle of Jesus Christ. He had his first vision at the age of twelve, and at twenty set out to establish his new religion. Mani, the founder of Manichaeism, wanted to establish a universal religion, and he took some parts from various religions of the world, both of the West and the East. Mani proclaimed himself as the fulfillment of the work of Zoroaster, Buddha, and Jesus.

Mani in India

Mani was a missionary. Mani's proper public activity did not have its beginning, as might be expected, in Mesopotamia, but in India.[5] He himself tells of it in a Coptic text: "At the close of King Ardashir's year, I set out to preach. I sailed to the land of the Indians. I preached to them the hope of life and I chose there a good selection." Probably knowing the legend of St. Thomas and perhaps inspired by his example, Mani went to India by ship as did once the Apostle Thomas. But the voyage is likely to have taken him no farther than the Iranian provinces of Turan and Makran as well as Northwestern India, Gandhara (i.e., to these regions now comprising Pakistan). Mani spent over a year in India. During his stay in India, he would have known not only Buddhism, but also Jainism. Manichaeism (Manikhayya) means the vessel of life. "Mani" means vessel or container. The word Mani is interpreted as "shedding manna."[6]

Manichaeism is a Gnostic religion based on the dual forces of good and evil. Now only a few thousand people follow this religion. Bahram I did not like Mani. He chained him and put him into prison, where he remained for twenty-six days without food and drink. At the end of the twenty-sixth day, he died, aged fifty-eight years.

The Five Ethical Principles or Commandments of Mahavira to Jain Monks (Ascetics)

The Jain Community is fourfold, Monks and Nuns; lay brothers and lay sisters. Mahavira, the reformer of Jainism in the Sixth Century B.C., prescribed five ethical principles to his Monks. They are called the five commandments or the five great vows (Mahavrata). They are as follows.

1. Non-violence or non-injury (Ahimsa)
2. Speaking the truth (Satya)
3. Non-stealing (Asteya)

4. Purity or celibacy (Brahmacarya): purity in word, thought and deed
5. Non-possession (Aparigraha)[7]

The Five Commandments of Mani to the Elect or the Chosen

Mani divided the Manichee believers into two groups, designating the first group the elect or chosen, and the second group the hearers. In both groups there were males and females. Mani gave five commandments or ethical principles to the elect or the chosen. They are as follows:

1. Truthfulness
2. Non-injury
3. Celibacy (chastity)
4. Purity of mouth, hand, and sex
5. No possession or property[8]

When we place side by side these five ethical principles of Mahavira and Mani, we could see clearly where the source comes from: Who has influenced whom? Definitely Mani, who lived in the third century A.D., was influenced by Mahavira who lived in the sixth century B.C.

When we look into the order of these five ethical principles, Mahavira states as the first ethical principle, non-injury or non-violence, whereas Mani places it as the second. That which Mahavira places as the second ethical principle, speaking the truth, Mani places as the first. When Mahavira places purity in thought, word, and deed, or celibacy, as the fourth ethical principle, Mani places celibacy as the third ethical principle and elaborates it as purity of mouth, hand, and sex as the fourth ethical principle. He has left aside the third ethical principle of non-stealing. The fifth ethical principle Mahavira gives to his monks is non-possession. Mani also places it as the fifth.

Mani seems, therefore, to have borrowed these five ethical principles from Jainism, as far as form is concerned.

Now let us turn to the content of these five ethical principles from the side of Mahavira and Mani.

1. Non-Violence or Non-Injury (Ahimsa)

According to Mahavira, non-killing or Ahimsa is the cornerstone of Jainism. On this ethical principle the other four ethical principles rest. Non-injury is the heart, soul, and root of Jainism. It is considered as the supreme virtue and religion of Jainism. The other four ethical principles are merely corollaries of Ahimsa. Ahimsa may thus be generalized as the fundamental ethical virtue of Jainism; judgment on all actions may be passed in accordance with the standard of Ahimsa; speaking the truth, non-stealing, celibacy, and non-possession are regarded as virtues, as their transgression leads to himsa (injury to beings).[9] The Jain monks were commanded to be the strict followers of this virtue of non-injury or Ahimsa. It is worth noting here Mahatma Gandhi was very much influenced by Jainism. For his non-violent movement he took the first two ethical principles of Jainism, namely non-violence and speaking the truth, Ahimsa and Sathya-graha (holding to the truth). The term "A-himsa" literally means non-killing. There are two aspects to Ahimsa. One is negative, the other is positive. Negative aspects include not to allow or commit violence in any form and to prevent the committing of violence. Its positive aspects include compassion, kindness, help, charity, etc. The term "Ahimsa" includes also five-sensed living organisms.

7

Jainism, from its very inception, proclaimed that life (Jiva or Soul) exists even at micro levels, in infinitesimally small organisms invisible to the naked eye as well as in the larger vegetable, animal, and human organisms. We are surrounded by billions of such Jivas and every action that causes injury to any Jiva is returned to the person who inflicts that injury. Jainism commands "Love all life," not only human life but also animal and vegetable life.[10] Non-injury is considered as the highest form of religion. In Hemachandra's words, non-injury is "the beneficent mother of all beings," the elixir for those who wander in suffering through the ocean of reincarnation. The positive Ahimsa is expressed in the form of giving protection to all living creatures.[11]

Mani also gave to his elect (the chosen) the ethical principle of non-injury to be practiced. The demands of non-injury expected from the elect were severe too.

Like the Jain monks, the elect (chosen) were vegetarians. They abstained from meat, marriage, and property. Their obligation not to produce fresh life or to take it was so absolute that it extended to the vegetable kingdom. "They might neither sow nor reap, nor even break their bread themselves, lest they pain the light which was mixed with it."[12] Manichaeism was always ascetic, even to the terms in which Mani expressed his cosmology. All generation was to Mani hateful, for it was a fresh mixture. To take life was to cut off the parts of the light imprisoned in a living body.

In the confessions "Khuastuanift," fifteen kinds of sins are enumerated. The offenses are committed against five kinds of animals: man, quadrupeds, flying animals, and (lowest of all) things that creep on the earth. "My God, these five kinds . . . should we ever have frightened or scared, beaten or struck, angered or pained them, or killed them"—then we must say Manastar Hirza.[13]

Even though they are the confessions of the hearers, they are applicable to the elect (chosen) as well, since they have to observe the ethical principle of non-injury very seriously.

The five divine elements—air, wind, light, water, fire—which formed the panoply of the primal man, were unable to return to heaven and are now upon this earth, where they give radiancy, light, and consistency to the things they produce. If the Manichees harmed them, they must ask pardon. The Manichees held in reverence the five divine elements and anything that would force them from their imprisonment in "dark" matter it was their duty to do. Equally, it was a Manichees's duty to do anything that tended still further to imprison these elements.[14] St. Augustine is very critical of the Manichee ethics. The sympathy of the Manichee was directed not towards men, but towards the light imprisoned in men. They are not concerned about persons but with things.[15]

The Jains believe there are *Jivas* or *souls* in the five elements and we must not harm them.[16] Manichees believe there are *particles of light* in the five elements and we must not harm them.

2. Speaking the Truth (Satya)

The second ethical principle is speaking the truth. In the case of the householder the strict observance of this commandment is not insisted on, but it is strongly insisted on for the Jain monks. The vow of truthfulness requires the Jain monk to be free of anger, greed, fear, and delusion, so that anything he utters is free from the taint of impurity of any kind.[17]

Mani insisted on truthfulness to his elect. He insisted so much, he made it as their first ethical principle. He also made some exception to this rule. Since Manichaeism was very much persecuted during the time of Mani, if the elect were caught and questioned whether they were Manichaeists, they could say, "We are not Manichaeists," and escape. The enemies tricked the Manichaeists by releasing ants. They would tell them to kill the ants. If they killed the ants, the enemy would know that they were not Manichaeists and would set them free. If they did not kill the ants, they would be persecuted. During the Eucharistic celebration, if they refused to drink wine, they would be caught as Manichaeists. So they were allowed to use their discretion.

The Jain Monks were always very strict in observing the second ethical principle of speaking the truth always. One should respect the vow of truthfulness, by *always* avoiding jesting, greed, cowardice, and anger, and by thinking before speaking.[18]

3. Non-Stealing (Asteya)

This virtue signifies the strict adherence to one's own possessions—not even wanting to take hold of another's. All the evil practices observed in trade and commerce such as adulterating the materials and not giving others their money's worth, not weighing or measuring properly and indulging in black marketing constitutes stealing (stea). Mahavira places "non-stealing" as the third ethical principle to his monks, whereas Mani does not give this ethical principle to his elect.

4. Purity of Celibacy (Brahmacarya) (Purity in Word, Thought, and Deed)

In the case of Jain monks, this virtue of chastity signifies complete abstinence from sex. Abstention is certainly applied to the act, but even thoughts entertained about sex were

10

considered to be undesirable, and as bad and unethical as the sexual act itself. The principle of coordination of thought, word, and deed is applicable to the principle of celibacy as well. This ethical principle also commands that a Jain monk should not take *any food which is likely to incite his passion.* He should not think of any woman nor give any cause by talk or gesture to excite passion in himself or in the woman. He should not try to relive his past sexual contacts.[19]

What Mahavira gave to his Jain monks as the fourth ethical principle, Mani splits into two ethical principles. Celibacy (third) and purity of mouth, hand, and sex (fourth). The elect were complete celibates like the Jain monks. This ethical principle of Mani can be summarized in the three famous signacula that St. Augustine mentions in chapter 10 of his publication, *De Moribus Manichaeorum: Signaculum Oris* (Signet or purity of the mouth) *Signaculum Manuum* (Signet or purity of the hand) and *Signaculum Sinus* (Signet or purity of sex). These three signets denoted a comprehensive range, for "os" implied all the *five senses,* "manus" implied all *behavior,* and "sinus" implied every expression of *sexual urge* (*omnis libido seminalis*).

The purity of mouth included cleanliness or purity of thought and word—above all, restraint from utterance of any kind that could seem in Manichaean teaching to breathe blasphemy. At the same time, this precept held good without restriction for whatever could be enjoyed by way of the mouth. Just like Mahavira advised his monks to avoid certain kinds of food that may arouse their sex feelings, Mani's wish to his elect was that they should abstain from whatever could strengthen the body's sensual lusts.

The purity of the hand prescribed by Mani to his elect, above all, was the prohibition of any action that could harm plant and animal life. Manichees were not allowed to uproot any plant nor kill any animal life. A notable fact is that according to Manichaean outlook those who sinned against this precept sustained a punishment corresponding to their criminal transaction.

> He who mowed the sown field would himself be born again as an ear of corn, whilst he who killed a mouse would in future life be a mouse, and so on. [20]

Even among Jains they do not work in the fields as agriculturalists and farmers for fear of hurting any insects. Most of the Jains are traders and businessmen. They belong to the prosperous class of the Vaishya community.

5. Non-possessions (Aparigraha)

Mahavira gave this ethical principle of non-possession to his Jain monks. The monk must renounce all his property and wealth. But the mere physical renunciation is not of much value. He must also have no thoughts whatever of the things renounced. Because of their constant association with him, it is very likely that thoughts about his former possessions may linger on his mind. The monk has to combat the tendency to retrospect about what he no longer possesses. The attitude of detachment towards everything is to be adhered to. Aparigraha or non-attachment does not only mean non-attachment to external objects and property but includes non-attachment to the body or its requirements. He must annihilate his desires and should attach greater importance to the body than to regard it as an instrument for practice of dharma and realization of the three jewels (right faith, right knowledge, and right conduct). Even the three articles which he is permitted to possess, namely a book (jñaopadhi), a peacock-feather bunch (samya mopadhi) and a pot for water normally made of wood (sancopādhi) should have no attraction for him. In short, he should have an attitude of non-attachment, complete and thorough, both for sentient and non-sentient objects.[21]

Like Mahavira gave to his Jain Monks the rule of not owning anything, Mani also gave to the elect the rule of not possessing anything or any property. They were supposed to live a wandering life, possessing no more than food for a day and clothes for a year.[22]

From our research, we conclude that Mani owes very much to Mahavira and to Jainism for his ethical thought on non-injury.

Now let us turn to the *practices* of Jainism and Manichaeism. Under this section we shall discuss the *food, drink, customs,* and *habits* of these two religions.

Food

Food and non-injury (Ahimsa) have a close relationship. Ahimsa (non-injury) necessarily requires taking of vegetarian food. Some go still further and live only on fruits, these being called "fruitarians"[23] in India. The Jain scriptures, deploring the almost universal habit of eating meat, attach great importance to dietary rules. The widespread vegetarian diet of present-day India is very much the result of the Jains' emphasis on the evils of destroying animal life for sport, food, or sacrifice. On the other hand, the Brahmanic schools condone animal sacrifices and even approve of certain meat dishes on particular occasions. The Jains were extremely critical of the Buddhists being allowed to eat meat on the ground that they themselves did not kill the animals but that they were getting the meat from the butchers. The Jains' view is that but for the meat eaters, the butchers themselves would not indulge in the evil act of killing the animals and that such meat eaters are indirectly responsible for killing.

The purity of mouth, pertaining to eating meat and drinking liquor, is observed very strictly by the Jains. They would not eat meat, even though they did not kill the animals, which others killed and provided.

Even in their vegetarian diet, Jains, as they advance to the higher stages of their spiritual career, called pratimas, are expected to avoid certain varieties of food, notably fruits with many seeds and fermented products of milk, and to refrain from eating after sunset, lest they cause injury to the innumerable insects that come to life at dusk. For the same reason, the means of livelihood open to a devout Jain exclude professions that involve destruction of plants, use of fire and poisonous stuffs, and trade connected with slavery and animal husbandry. This accounts for the fact that the Jains, today as in the ancient days, are mostly to be found in the middle classes of Vaishya rank, the merchant castes of India.[24] The Jains also do not eat honey.

The food of the "elect" of the Manichees is fruits and vegetables. They enjoyed light fruits, such as watermelons and cucumbers. They liked strong vegetables, i.e., raw vegetables. Cooking could harm the light that is in the vegetable. So they ate raw vegetables, and fruits.

But the chosen (*electi*) of the Manichees were not as strict as the Jain monks. They made excuses. The partaking of these foods were accompanied by an express declaration of guiltlessness of the *electi*. The *Acta Archelai*, chapter 10, repeats the formula applied to the consumption of bread.

> I did not mow thee, did not grind thee, nor knead, nor lay thee in the oven, but another did do this and bring thee to me, I eat without sin.[25]

Drink

Just as the Jain monks were forbidden spirits or liquor, so the Manichee elect were also forbidden to drink wine or liquor. The use of oil was highly approved for the elect. For drink, fruit juices were the first choice. Larger quantities of water had to be avoided by them because water is a material substance.[26] According to Jainism, the cold water is believed to contain souls or *jivas* and, therefore, *sadhus*. Jain monks may not use it except if they strain the water with a piece of cloth and drink it.[27]

Customs

Jain monks shaved their heads, while Mani's elect grew hair and wore hats. Jain monks sweep the ground as they go for fear of hurting any insects. When walking, they cover their mouths with a piece of cloth for fear of inhaling living organisms. Among Jain monks, many reject the use of loudspeakers to avoid violence to the air souls or beings (*jivas*).[28]

The Habit—"White-Clad Ones" and "Sky-Clad Ones"

There were two sects of Jain monks. Those who wore white garments were called White-Clad Ones—*Svetambara*—which means those whose garment is white (*ambara*, garment, *sveta*, white). This raiment denoted their ideal of alabaster-like purity. In Mahavira's period many Jain monks assumed white garments for the sake of decency and called themselves *White-Clad Ones*.[29] The other sect was known as the *Sky-Clad Ones*

(*Digambara*). In ancient times the Jain monks went about completely naked, having put away all those caste marks and particularizing tokens that are the essence of Indian costume, symbolizing the wearer's involvement in the web of human bondage. The *Tirthankaras* or Jain supreme teachers are therefore sometimes depicted naked and sometimes clad in white. Here we are dealing with the *White-Clad Ones* only.

Manichees were also called *White-Clad Ones*.[30] Even though Brahmins, Magi, Mandaeans, Syrian priests at Duro-Europos wore white garments,[31] they were not called "White-Clad Ones." Manichees wore long white robes and Mani used the Jain term *White-Clad Ones* for his chosen or the elect.

It is our finding that Manichaeism is very much indebted to Jainism for its ethical principles and especially for Ahimsa (non-injury or non-violence), and for the white garments worn by the *White-Clad Ones*.

Notes

1. Geoffrey Parrinder, *World Religions—From Ancient History to the Present*, Jainism, Chapter 14. Facts on File Publications, New York, 1934, p. 241.

2. Thomas J. Hopkins, *The Hindu Religious Tradition,* Wadsworth Publishing Co., Belmont, California, 1971, p. 54.

3. S. Radhaknishnan, *Indian Philosophy*, Vol. 1, New York, 1922, p. 286.

4. Colette Caillat, *Jainism, Encyclopedia of World Religions.* Mircea Eliade, p. 514.

5. Geo. Widengren, *Mani and Manichaeism,* Widenfeld and Nicholson, London, 1965, pp. 96-97.

6. Jes Asmussen, *Xuastvanift, Studies in Manichaeism*, Copenhagen, 1965.

7. Mrs. Sinclair Stevenson, *The Heart of Jainism,* Milford, 1915, pp. 234-238.

8. Gherardo Gnoli, "Manichaeism" in *Encyclopedia of World Religions,* Mircea Eliade, p. 167.

9. Surendranath Dasgupta, *History of Indian Philosophy*. University Press, Cambridge, 1922, pp. 199-201.

10. Dr. M. M. Kothari, "The Positive Content in the Concept of Non-Violence" (in *Perspectives in Jaina Philosophy and Culture*), Ahimsa International, New Delhi, ed. Jain and Sogani, 1985.

11. William R., *Jaina Yoga*, pp. 37-38. Oxford University Press, London (Quotation) T. K. Tukol, *Compendium of Jainism,* Prasarange, Karnataka, University Dharwad, India, 1980, p. 208.

12. F. C. Burkitt. *The Religion of the Manichees*, University Press, Cambridge, 1925, p. 45.

13. Ibid., p. 53.

14. Mrs. Sinclair Stevenson, op. cit. p. 235.

15. Ibid., p. 258.

16. Geo. Widengren, *Mani and Manichaeism*, Widenfeld and Nicholson, London, 1965, pp. 96-97.

17. T. K. Tukol, op. cit., pp. 258-259.

18. Mrs. Sinclair Stevenson, op. cit., p. 235.

19. T. K. Tukol, op. cit., p. 258.

20. Geo. Widengren, op. cit., p. 97.

21. T. K. Tukol., op. cit., p. 259.

22. F. C. Burkitt, op. cit., p. 45.

23. Dr. M. M. Kothari, op. cit., p. 28.

24. Ibid., p. 29.

25. Geo. Widengren, op. cit., p. 97.

26. Ibid., p. 25.

27. Dr. Herman Jacobi, *On Jainism,* Hirachand Nemehand Doshi Sholapur, India, 1914, p. 22.

28. Dr. M. M. Kothari, op. cit., p. 28.

29. Heinrich Zimmer, ed. Joseph Campbell, *Philosophies of India.* Bollinger, Princeton, New Jersey, 1974, p. 210.

30. Jason Beduhn, at the class lecture on Manichaeism, March 8, 1989, before Prof. Richard Frye and his students, class "Mesopotamian and Iranian Religions from Alexander the Great to Muhammed."

31. Geo. Widengren, op. cit., p. 25.

Bibliography

Asmussen, Jes P., *Xuastvanift, Studies in Manichaeism,* Copenhagen, 1965.

Burkitt, F. C. *The Religion of the Manichees,* University Press, Cambridge, 1925.

Caillat, Colette, "Jainism," Encyclopedia of World Religions, Mircea Eliade.

Dasgupta, Surendranath, *History of Indian Philosophy,* University Press, Cambridge, 1922.

Gnoli, Gherardo, "Manichaeism" in Encyclopedia of World Religions, Mircea Eliade.

Hopkins, Thomas J., *The Hindu Religious Tradition,* Wadsworth Publishing Co., Belmont, California, 1971.

Jacobi, Herman, *On Jainism,* Hirachand Nemehand Doshe Sholapur, India, 1914.

Kothari, M. M. "The Positive Content in the Concept of Non-Violence" (in *Perspectives in Jaina Philosophy and Culture*), Ahimsa International, New Delhi, ed. Jain and Sogani, 1985.

Parrinder, *World Religions—From Ancient History to the Present,* Facts on File Publications, New York, 1984.

Radhaknishnan, S., *Indian Philosophy,* vol. 1, New York, 1922.

Stevenson, Mrs. Sinclair, *The Heart of Jainism,* Milford, 1915.

Tukol, T. K., *Compendium of Jainism*, Prasaranga, Dharwad, India, 1980.

Widengren, Geo., *Mani and Manichaeism*, Widenfeld and Nicholson, London, 1965.

William, R., *Jaina Yoga,* Oxford University Press, London.

Zimmer, Heinrich, ed. Joseph Campbell, *Philosophies of India*, Bolliger, Princeton, New Jersey, 1974.

Part II

Chapter 2

Caste in Hinduism

The Vedic Society and the author of the book of "Manu" tell us how the gods created the castes in the society.

They created four classes. These are:

1. Brahmins—those of contemplative nature, spiritually inspired and inspiring
2. Kshatriyas—those whose talents are administrative, executive, and protective
3. Vaisyas—those who serve through skill, agriculture, trade, commerce, and business life in general
4. Sudras—those capable of offering service to society through bodily labor

Some classify these four classes into priests, soldiers, farmers, and servants. The word used for the four great classes is *varna* which is Sanskrit for *color*. The first mention of the *varnas* is found in the *Purusha-Sukta* of Rig-Veda; where it is said that the *Brahmins* issued from the mouth of *Purusha*, the primal giant, the *Kshatriyas* or warriors from his arms, the *Vaisyas* or peasants from his thighs, and the *Sudras* or serfs from his feet.

The Vedic Society thought it was good and wholesome to have these four classes in order to maintain law and order in the society. What the Veda calls "RTA," which means right order and truth, the later texts were to call *Dharma.* The basis of the Hindu way of life used to be considered the so-called *Varnasrma-Dharma,* the *Dharma* of class and the stages of life. This caste duty is clearly illustrated in Bhagavad-Gita. In the battlefield of *Kurushetra,* Arjuna refused to fight as a soldier against *Pandavas,* his own people. Krishna reminded him of his duty as a soldier and encouraged him to do his caste duty. "This honorable field—a *Kshatriya*—if, knowing thy duty and the task, thou bidd'st duty and task go by—that shall be sin!" (B.G. 2)

I cannot agree with the caste system in Hinduism. It is set up by the high class in order to dominate and control the lower class. It is very inhuman. The privileged class organized this caste system to their own benefit. I will not consider a Brahmin born in a Brahmin community to be superior to Sudra, who is born in a lower community.

A person should be judged by his morality, character, accomplishments, and service to the society, and not by birth.

Even today in India thousands and thousands of people are discriminated against in obtaining government positions because they do not belong to a higher class. They may have better qualifications and credentials, but just because they are born in a low caste family, they do not get the desired jobs. Prafulla Mohanti, in his book, *My Village, My Life,* portrays a low class boy who was qualified but could not get a job because of his caste. Here I quote the lines from Mohanti: "In the adjoining village Pahali Sahu had got his degree in arts but couldn't get a job for five years because he came from the oilmen's community. Whereas Nanda Kishore Bal got a job as an inspector of schools as soon as he got his B.A. That was because he was a Kshatriya." This is only an incident. There are hundreds of Pahali Sahus in India who are penalized because of their castes.

No one is superior by birth. Everyone is equal by birth. I like the aphorism of Thiruvalluvar. In his Kural he says that "All men that live are one in circumstances of both. Diversities of works give each his special worth." (Kural 972)

A Brahmin cannot boast that he is a superior being just because he is born in that class. Greatness is not his birthright. He must earn his greatness by performing service to the society.

The caste system is very absurd. Quoting again from Prafulla Mohanti's book, *My Village, My Life*: "High caste Hindus will take water from the hands of a barber but not from a washerman, who is considered untouchable. It is ironic that someone who is untouchable is the only person who can wash clothes to make them virtually pure." Now the caste system has become a canker in Hinduism. Great thinkers and sages of India have been fighting against caste systems for centuries. These great men thought that the mental attitude of people should be changed by good education. One such great man was Ambekkar. He was from a low caste. He fought against the evils of the caste system. He is known as the Father of the Indian Constitution, having written it.

In some Hindu temples, low caste Hindus were not allowed to enter the temple to worship their gods. Is it not shameful? When rats and mice could run around the idols, human beings could not even see the idols. By the efforts of Mohandas Gandhi, temples were opened for the outcastes. Gandhi called the untouchables the *harijans* (*Hari*—God, *jans*—people), the people of God. Gandhi said the British and untouchability kept India enslaved—the British politically, and untouchability morally. By treating the untouchables as unclean, the caste Hindus made themselves doubly unclean. (R. C. Zaehner, *Hinduism*, p. 173)

I believe with Gandhi that the ideal of caste should not be the caste system but conscience and compassion. Gandhi said, "To me God is truth and love; God is ethics and morality; God is fearlessness. God is the source of light and life, and yet he is above and beyond all these. God is conscience." (R. C. Zaehner, op. cit., p. 171) M. Gandhi said, the duty of the enlightened Hindu is to preserve in it all that might be preserved, but to root out whatever offended his social conscience. From this statement we could conclude Gandhi was against the caste system. Gandhi's attitude to Hinduism was that it is the Dharma of India. "Yes! The Dharma of the Brahmins had yielded to the Dharma of conscience and compassion." (R. C. Zaehner, op. cit., p. 174) Gandhi saw a difference between caste and Varna, calling caste "a travesty of Varna that has degraded Hinduism in India."[1]

The high caste Hindu will not drink water from the well used by an outcaste Hindu. The shadow of an outcaste Hindu cannot fall on a high caste Hindu. He should walk far away from him. We are created to the image and likeness of God. How foolish it is to treat our fellow man like this! As Swami Vivekananda says, "I have the same God in me as you have in you. That is what we want, no privilege for anyone, equal chances for all; let everyone be taught that the divine is within, and everyone will work out his own salvation." (From the complete works of Swami Vivekananda 3:245-46.)

In the United States of America and in Europe, everyone does different kinds of jobs. We have teachers, barbers, cleaners, farmers, blue-collar workers, priests, cooks, and so many other jobholders. We do not label them as low castes and high castes. We esteem and honor every kind of job. We know the dignity of labor. The different services of different people are necessary for the functioning of society. This idea of "nobility of work" should be propagated among our Hindu brothers and sisters in India.

It is worth quoting the words of Sri Ramakrishna Paramavahansa: "The caste system can be removed by one means only and that is the love of God. Lovers of God do not belong to any caste. The mind, body, and soul of a man becomes purified through divine love. Chaitanya and Nityanada scattered the name of Hari to everyone, including the pariah (lowest class), and embraced them all. A Brahmin without this love is no longer a Brahmin, and a pariah (lowest class) with the love of God is no longer a pariah. Through Bhakti, an untouchable becomes pure and elevated." (*The Gospel of Ramakrishna,* p. 86)

There is awakening among Hindus. They do not want to be stuck with the old caste system, but prefer change, a new way of life. As Mohanti says, "For common colds the usual treatment was honey and ginger with tulashi leaves. Now there are these long capsules which you can buy. Nobody wants to suffer anymore. They all want instant cures. Before, when caste system prevailed, it was the age of darkness. Nobody is looking back. People are now enlightened. They are all looking forward." (Prafulla Mohanti, op. cit., p. 26)

It is the society that created the caste system, but every person longs to live in unity and peace. Even though Jagannath Satpathi is a Brahmin, he wishes that everyone in his village would be one in mind and heart. His innermost feelings are expressed in this manner. "It would be a nice place to live in if people didn't quarrel and there was no jealousy and people shared their sorrows and happiness." (Mohanti, op. cit., p. 31) At the same time, Asoka Panda, a Brahmin boy, likes to play with other boys and to be equal with them, but Brahmin society does not permit that. He is told that his caste is the best caste and he is different from other boys. He suffers emotionally and is unable to express his feelings.

Jagu, the weaver, indirectly tells us how the Hindus want a change in their caste system. They are fed up with the old system. The old system has to give way to a new way of life. "But people don't want our fabrics anymore. They all want mill-made saris with colorful prints. They like nylon and dacron which we didn't know about in our childhood." (Mohanti, op cit., p. 167)

Alani Rana is a potter. He is considered untouchable, yet his pots are used in the kitchen, the most sacred place in the house. Alani Rana is telling us in the old days he used to sell a lot of pots but now, in every house, they are using metal pots for cooking. Yes, clay pots of caste systems must give way to the metal pots of equality, love, compassion, peace, and harmony in the Hindu society. Gandhi went about in a loincloth till every Harijan (untouchable, or people of God) in India gets decent cloth to wear. He longed to see the day when a Harijan would be a prime minister of India. Gandhi said, "If I have to be reborn, I would wish to be born an untouchable so that I might share their sorrows, their sufferings, and the affronts leveled on them in order that I might endeavor to free myself and them from this miserable condition." (F. G. Herod, *World Religions,* p. 14)

Steps are being taken to abolish the untouchability in India. The outcastes are now known as the *scheduled* castes and they have their own representatives in Parliament. This is the beginning of a change of attitude which will take many years, if not centuries, to spread through the whole of India.

In this century, in Tamil Nadu, South India, there arose a famous social reformer called E. V. Ramasamy, popularly known as "Periyar". He traveled all through India speaking and writing against the evils of the caste system and founded a movement called "Dravida-Kazaham" (D.K.).

In Tamil Nadu, in recent years, many movies were released portraying the evils of the caste system. One famous movie was *Passi (Hunger)*, which was released in 1979, directed by Dorai. In this movie, the condition of low-class people in the slums is depicted. The evils of the caste systems are condemned.

Another movie was *Thannir, Thannir* (in Tamil this means *Water, Water*), released in 1980, directed by K. Balachandrar. In this movie, too, the evils of the caste system are attacked.

The caste system is like a cancer in the society. It is like a leprosy in the Hindu land. It is like the modern day "AIDS" in the Hindu community. It should be eradicated. No man is an island. Each one needs the other. A priest needs the people. A weaver needs the carpenter, and a ruler needs the farmer. Everyone is our brother and sister who can build this world into a better place to live.

Let the caste system fade away from Hindu society. Let love, peace and DHARMA rule the Hindu society.

Note

1. In its ideal form, Gandhi supported the Varna System. In 1927 he said, "Man shall follow the profession of his ancestors for earning his livelihood." He went on to describe caste as "An inscrutable law of nature discovered by Hindu law that encouraged self-restraint and conservation of energy for service and spiritual matters."

Chapter 3

Childbirth in India

Every woman finds her fulfillment by being a mother. This is a psychological instinct implanted in every woman. In India, where women enjoy fewer privileges than men, women take more pride in bringing forth children. Doranne Jacobson, writing about childbirth, describes it as "the one thing without which no kin group or society could long exist." The Tamils in South India call it as "childblessing." In Tamil it is *makkad-perru*. Women in India like to bring forth children, especially male children. Doranne Jacobson and Katherine Mayo bring out these ideas in their respective articles. Now let me turn to the articles of Doranne Jacobson, "Golden Handprints and Red-Painted Feet: Hindu Childbirth Rituals in Central India," and Katherine Mayo, "Mother India."

In these two articles, the authors present their views and interpretations of Indian childbirth to the Western world. They wrote their articles in different times. Katherine Mayo wrote her article in 1926. Doranne Jacobson researched hers in the 1960's and 1970's. One can see very clearly in their articles the differences in time factor, milieu, sanitary conditions, customs, and beliefs while treating the same theme—childbirth.

No wonder Katherine Mayo's description of childbirth is crude and horrible. She describes the atrocity committed by the midwife (Dhai) against a woman who dies in childbirth in this manner:

> First she brings pepper and rubs it into the dying eyes, that the soul may be blinded and unable to find its way out. Then she takes two long iron nails, and, stretching out her victim's unresisting arms, for the poor creature knows and accepts her fate, drives a spike straight through each palm fast, into the floor. This is done to pinion the soul to the ground, to delay its passing or that it may not rise and wander, vexing and living. And so the woman dies, piteously calling for the gods for pardon for those black sins of a former life for which she is suffering.[1]

I find a note of pessimism in the article of Katherine Mayo. During her time, medical facilities did not reach many villages in India. Superstitions and ignorance were widespread in many villages.

During the time Doranne Jacobson visited India, midwives in the village of Nimkhara had received some training in modern methods and sterile techniques at the district hospitals, but in practice the midwives ignored their training. Nurses are called only in extreme cases. The villagers go to midwives because their methods are more familiar and the traditional midwives' fees are lower than the government nurses' fees. I find a note of optimism in Doranne's article.

The two writers are of the same mind when they tell us that the Hindu society considers a woman in childbirth as unclean. She is polluted and kept separate from the rest of the family. Doranne uses the Hindu term for the woman in labor, *Jachcha*, which means polluted and polluting state.

Katherine Mayo and Doranne Jacobson agree that the room where the woman in labor is placed is dirty and with dim light. Whereas Katherine Mayo very poignantly describes the condition of the room of the expectant mother in the following way:

> And it is into this evil-smelling rubbish hole that the young wife creeps when her hour is come upon her. "Unclean" she is, in her pain—unclean whatever she touches, and fit thereafter to be destroyed . . . . If there be a broken-legged, ragged string-cot, let her have that to lie upon . . . . [2]

Both authors speak about the role of midwives and their importance in child delivery. Yet, they are considered as untouchables and poorly paid for their jobs. Katherine Mayo discusses at length the character and the role of the midwife.

The action of the midwife is described in detail by Katherine Mayo as follows:

> She kneads the patient with her fist; stands her against the wall and butts her head; props her upright on the bare ground, seizes her hands and shoves against her thighs with gruesome bare feet, until, the doctors state, the patient's flesh is often torn to ribbons, by the Dhai's long, ragged toenails. Or, she lays the woman flat and walks up and down her body, like one treading grapes. [3]

Doranne Jacobson writes that the woman in labor must not cry out or shout. In childbirth, as in other facets of life, restraint is the keynote. The woman in labor must keep her emotions under control. Katherine Mayo does not say anything about it.

At the time of delivery, Katherine Mayo mentions the objects used by the midwife. They are hollyhock roots, dirty string, rags full of quince seeds, earth mixed with cloves, butter and marigold flowers, nuts, spices, goats' hair, scorpions' stings, monkey skulls, snakeskins, split bamboo, old tin can, rusty nail, potsherds, fragments of broken glass, coin and knife.

Doranne Jacobson mentions sickle and razor blades as used by the midwife at the time of delivery to cut out the umbilical cord.

The villagers of Nimkhara have strong belief in their gods. The Jachcha may be fed with water in which the idols in the village temple have been bathed. The sacred water is said to alleviate labor pains and bring about a speedy delivery.

I think Doranne Jacobson and Katherine Mayo have succeeded in telling the Western world about the atrocities committed by midwives in India. Now in India medical facilities are improving. Doctors and nurses are thriving in India. Hospitals are using new techniques and new methods in child deliveries.

Notes

1. Katherine Mayo, *Mother India*, pages 101-102.
2. Katherine Mayo, op. cit., page 91.
3. Katherine Mayo, op. cit., page 93.

Chapter 4

Image Worship or Idolatry

People of India are God-conscious by nature. They see and feel the presence of God in every object of creation. This idea is well brought out in the Tamil literature *Thirumuruhattupaddai* pertaining to Lord Muruga. The devotee of Lord Muruga sees Him in every object of creation and praises Him in the following words:

> You are the spark in the fire!
> You are the nectar in the flower!
> You are the truth in the words!
> You are the diamond in the stones!

The Western mind cannot fully understand the nature and the framework of the Eastern mind which is basically religious. Without understanding the spirit of Indian religions, Westerners label the Easterners as idolators and image worshipers. It is not fair and very deplorable.

The Hindus not only saw God in every object of creation but they also imagined Him in deep contemplation and meditation. Then they gave forms to these images they had conceived in their minds. The sculptors and metalworkers, when they made the images, believed that the images had protective significances. The Vedic hymns were designed to persuade the gods to deal generously with men.

> As birds extend their sheltering wings,
> Spread your protection over us.
>
> Rigveda

We know that God is infinite. With our finite mind we cannot comprehend Him. We try to know Him through His creation. While trying to know Him, mankind has given Him different names and forms.

The Tamil Saint Manickavacahar in his world renowned devotional book, Thiruvacaham, explains this thought very well.

> To the One who has no name,
> To the One who has no form,
> Let us call Him by thousand names
> And praise Him.
> "Thiruvempavai"
>
> In Thiruvacaham

It is sad scholars like Ralph Fitch, Mark Twain, and Erasmus, with their Western background and culture have failed to perceive the inner meaning behind these images. They could only write such things as, "They have their images standing . . . made of stone and wood, some like lions, leopards, and monkeys . . . "(Ralph Fitch, 1584), "wild mob of nightmares" (Mark Twain).

When the Hindus bow before sticks and stones, they do not understand them as sticks and stones. As Diane L. Eck writes in her book, *Darsan*, idolatry can be only an outsider's term for the symbols and visual images of some other culture.

What is idolatry? It is very difficult to define idolatry. In the past we thought making images of the sun, moon, and creatures, and worshipping them as God was idolatry.

St. Paul widens the old religious conception and makes it include all practices which are tantamount to a *dethronement of God in favor of a creature.*

Any excessive attachment to gluttony, covetousness, and money is idolatry (Eph. 5:5, Philippians 3:19). In another place, St. Paul writes, "Their stomach is their God."

To those who make fun of Indian religions and their adherents, and only call them idolators, I could turn around and tell them they are also idolators (technological idolators). Their redemption and literature depend upon material objects, namely machines and gadgets. Technological idolatry is the religion whose doctrines are explicity or implicity promulgated in the advertising pages of newspapers and magazines, TV, radio, the source from which millions of men, women, and children in the capitalist countries now derive their philosophy of life. In Soviet Russia during the years of its industrialization, technological idolatry was promoted almost to the rank of a state religion. Military success depends very largely on machines. Because this is so, machines tend to be credited with the power of bringing success in every sphere of activity, of solving all problems, social and personal, as well as military and technical.

It is less harmful to bow before sticks and stones than to bow before machines and gadgets.

When we went to *Iskcon* (International Krishna Temple) on November 16, 1988, and saw the images of Krishna and Radha, I was not disturbed. I am quite used to seeing them in India for nine years and in Sri Lanka from my childhood. Once you discover the meanings behind the images, you will feel quite comfortable. A beginner may gain a different impression.

Swami Vivekananda—Pro Image Worship

I agree with Swami Vivekananda that images are necessary for our worship. God is not inside the image. It is a method and a technique to put one in thought of God. Religion itself consists of the realization that symbols and images are all helps to religion.

Every book—the Bible, Vedas, and Koran—is full of the power of words. Certain words have wonderful power over mankind. Again, there are other forms known as symbols, also greatly influential upon the human mind. Symbols are a natural expression of thought. We think symbolically. All our words are but symbols of the thought behind. The thoughts bring the symbol outside. The symbol of Crucifixion—the *Cross*, the representation of the moon by a crescent, of the sun by a disk or a rayed face, the scales of justice, the bandage over the eyes of love, the aureoled hand coming forth from a cloud and brandishing a weapon, the *fish* in Greek (Ixθus)—Ikthus gives the anagram of Christ. "Every great historical religion except Judaism and Islam has attempted to express its legends and myths in images." (James Hastings, *Encyclopedia of Religion and Ethics*, page 111)

Even though image worship is the lowest form of worship, they are necessary aids to think of God. We are all spiritual babies. We must pass through the concrete. Children learn through the concrete first and gradually come to the abstract. If we tell a baby that five times two is ten, it will not understand, but if you bring ten things and show how five times two is ten, then the baby will understand. Swami Vivekananda is telling us that religion is a long, slow process. We may be old and have studied all the books in the universe, but we are all spiritual babies. We have learned the doctrines and dogmas, but realized nothing in our lives. We shall have to begin now in the

39

concrete through forms and words, ceremonies and images. Some require image outside. Some require image inside.

Image worship is something like little girls playing with dolls. Once they get married, they don't play with dolls, but cling to their husbands. In our spiritual journey, we go through images till we are realized in God.

Swami Dayamande Saraswati—Anti Image-Worship

Image is a help to worship. Some may be helped by images. Some may not. Saraswati's father forced Linga worship on his son. He did not give sufficient explanation. He told the son that the Lord Shiva is the idol. He should have told him it is only an *image* reminding of Shiva. At a tender age, he should not have forced the son to fast.

People who live in glass houses must not throw stones. As you have machines and gadgets, others have sticks and stones. As we have Lourdes, the Hindus have the sacred river Ganges.

Let us merit respect by respecting other people's religion.

Chapter 5

Loving Devotion (Bhagavad Gita)

Ravi and Puvi are living in Mambalam, Madras, South India. They have known each other from childhood. They played together and went to the same school together. In fact they are living on the same street. Ravi is now twenty-one years old and Puvi is seventeen years old. Ravi is from a poor family but Puvi is from a wealthy family. She is from Uddayar caste. This difference in their social status did not put an obstacle to their mutual love. Ravi and Puvi loved each other very much. Every evening Ravi would come to Puvi's house and offer her a jasmine flower (a white flower common in India) as a sign of his love.

Puvi liked flowers so much that she had her own garden in her backyard. She grew in the garden varieties of rose flowers and jasmine flowers. She watered them and took care of them with great pleasure. Now the flowers are blossoming. One red rose flower was in full bloom. Puvi was very much attracted by that single red rose flower.

Now Puvi was celebrating her eighteenth birthday. Relatives and friends began to assemble in Puvi's house to celebrate her birthday. Everyone has come with expensive gifts, but poor Ravi did not have any money to buy a decent present for his girlfriend. He was very much perplexed and disturbed. He did not know what to do. He got a bright idea. He went into the garden of Puvi. He saw one red rose flower fully blossomed. He plucked it and ran to Puvi's house. When he arrived at Puvi's house, he saw a long line of relatives and friends waiting with their presents to see Puvi. Ravi joined the group. The line began to move faster and faster towards Puvi. Everyone came with the presents and greeted Puvi. Now Ravi's turn came to see Puvi. There he stood before his beloved with the red rose flower. For a minute Puvi could not believe her eyes. That was the red rose flower she watered and cherished for weeks and weeks. Now it was in the hands of Ravi. Puvi looked into the eyes of Ravi. The four ravishing eyes sparkled many a time. Only heaven knows what they spoke. Then Ravi handed that red rose flower to Puvi with great love. Puvi knew that was her flower. She knew the depth of Ravi's love for her and how much that red rose flower meant to her. Puvi accepted that red rose flower.

Just like Ravi taking the flower from Puvi's garden and offering it to her, the devotees whatever they give to the Lord, they take it from God's garden, the world, and offer it to Him. All that we give is His. What he wants is our loving devotion and our dedicated hearts.

> Whatever man gives to me
> In true devotion;
> Fruit, or water,
> A leaf, a flower;
> I will accept it.
> That gift is love,
> His heart's dedication.
>
> Bhagavad Gita 9: 26

The text tells us that any person, whatever caste he may be in, is not barred from worshiping the Lord. Anyone can offer sacrifice to the Lord. No need of any intermediaries or priests. He is available to all.

Fruit, water, leaf, and flower are common things found all around the world. They are within the reach of all. Anyone can take them and offer them to the Lord. In India, when devotees worship the Lord, they offer fruit, water, leaf and flowers. In Tamil the word pūsai (Pū—flower, sai—make) means make flowers or offer flowers to the Lord.

The Lord accepts with loving devotion anything the devotee gives Him. What is required is sincere love and a pure heart.

As Jesus said, "A cup of water given in my name will not go without a reward."

O God, give me faith, devotion and love,
so that I may constantly chant Thy Holy name.
Let my heart overflow with Thy Love
Let me realize what ravishment is there in Thy name,
And let my being be firmly rooted in Thee.
Thou art the indwelling spirit; awake my soul;
And let that communion be constant.
Then, merciful God, Thy supreme light
will ever shine in my life.

Dadu

Loving devotion is the way to God. Love is the universal language of human hearts.

Chapter 6

The Concept of Non-Violence in Hinduism, Buddhism, and Christianity (Parallel Thoughts)

Introduction

Perhaps the oldest and most complex of all the religions of the world is Hinduism. It is probably the most tolerant of all religions. Hinduism has also been the source of many other religions like Jainism and Buddhism. It is not a missionary religion like Buddhism and Christianity.

The Hindu saw the universe as the manifestation of God's power and glory. In all the objects of creation, a Hindu saw the eyes, ears, hands, feet, and head of God. Hence, a Hindu started respecting and revering all the living things of the world. It is said in one of the oldest books of Hinduism—*The Code of Manu*—the life of the cattle is very sacred, and imposed penalties upon those who slaughtered them. Among the greatest of sins listed in this book is the killing of cows. For those who have committed this sort of crime, the remedy is to live with cows for a year, controlling his mind, studying the sacred scripture. Hinduism teaches compassion even to plants, birds, and animals. It is said once a king in India was going in a chariot and he saw a jasmine creeper (plant) looking for a place to spread its branches. The king got down from his chariot, gave the chariot to this jasmine creeper and went home walking. There was another king who saw a peacock shivering and trembling with cold. This king gave his cloak to the peacock and went home. All these may sound strange and absurd to us, but they tell us very vividly and clearly the compassionate heart of the Hindus. The theory of non-violence (respect for life) for Hindus evolved from small species to high species—viz., man.

When we turn to Buddhism, its founder, Buddha, was a man of compassion and non-violence. He went about through the streets of India preaching for the good of man and animals with a heart as wide as the ocean. He was the only man who was ever ready to give up his life for animals to stop a sacrifice. He once said to a king, "If the sacrifice of a lamb helps you to go to heaven, sacrificing a man will help you better. So sacrifice me." Buddha had compassion on a lamb to be slaughtered in the temple. Buddha's compassion is not confined to mankind. It was extended to all living beings. Through this act, Buddha gave to the world the doctrine of non-violence or ethics of compassion.

Now looking at Christianity and its founder, Jesus Christ, His whole life, teaching and ministry, is one of compassion and non-violence. No wonder Mahatma Gandhi called Jesus "The Prince of non-violence."

He left that place and went into their synagogue. A man with a shrivelled hand happened to be there, and they put this question to Jesus hoping to bring an accusation against Him. "Is it lawful to work a cure on the Sabbath?" He said in response, "Suppose one of you has a sheep and it falls into a pit on the Sabbath. Will he not take hold of it and pull it out? Well, think how much more precious a human being is than a sheep." (Matthew 12: 10–12) He is a good and gentle shepherd who will go after one lost sheep. Jesus loves all lives. "The bruised reed He will not crush. The smoldering wick He will not quench." (Matthew 12: 20–21)

His entry into Jerusalem on a donkey is a symbol that He is the King of non-violence. He is with the poor and the powerless. He is the voice of the voiceless who cannot speak for themselves in the face of injustice. Is it the way to speak to the High Priest? said one of the guards and gave a sharp blow to Jesus. Jesus replied, "If I said anything wrong, produce the evidence, but if I spoke the truth, why hit me?"

"I have come so that they may have life and have it more abundantly," said Jesus, and died for the salvation of mankind.

The inspiration, motivation and the spirit of non-violence are found in these great religions of Hinduism, Buddhism and Christianity.

Now I would like to highlight some of the parallel thoughts on non-violence found in the Sacred Scriptures of these religions.

Parallel Thoughts

Hinduism tells us that there is a divine spark in man. That we are tarred with the same brush and are children of one and the same creator, and as such, the divine powers within us are infinite. To slight a single human being is to slight those divine powers and thus to harm not only that being but, with him, the whole world. (*Manu*)

The Bible tells us that God created man in his own image and likeness. Then God said, "Let us make man in our image, after our likeness."

God created man in his image, in the divine image He created him, male and female He created them.

Genesis 1: 26, 27

Both Hinduism and Christianity agree that man has a divine spark in him. When we harm a man, a woman, or a child, we are tearing the image of God.

Arjuna in Hinduism, Buddha in Buddhism, and Christ in Christianity are against killing and violence. They speak about the evil consequences of violence.

Buddha gives ten punishments to those who kill. He says, "He who hunts with his weapons those who are harmless and pure shall soon fall into one of these ten evils:

1. Fearful pain
2. Infirmity
3. Loss of limbs
4. Terrible disease
5. Madness, the loss of the mind
6. The King's persecution
7. A fearful indictment
8. The loss of possessions
9. The loss of relations
10. Fire from heaven that may burn his house.

"And when the evil-doer is no more, then he is reborn in hell!" (Dhammapada 10: 137–140)

Buddha defines the truthfinder "As one who lays aside the sword."

When Peter slashed the ear of the servant of the high priest, Jesus told Peter, "Put back your sword where it belongs. Those who use the sword are sooner or later destroyed by it." (Matthew 26: 52)

Arjuna, the warrior, in the battlefield refuses to kill his kith and kin. He tells Krishna that he would prefer to be killed by them rather than kill them. Even though he is given dominion over three worlds, he will not kill them. He wants to remain unresisting and unarmed. These are the immortal words of Arjuna:

> Knower of all things
> Though they should slay me
> How could I harm them?
> I cannot wish it.
> Never, never,
> Not though it won me
> the throne of the three worlds;
> How much the less for
> earthly lordship!
>
> Evil they may be,
> Worst of the wicked,
> Yet if we kill them
> Our sin is greater;
> How could we dare spill
> the blood that unites us?
> Where is joy in
> the killing of kinsmen?"

B. G. 1: 35, 46

Hinduism, Buddhism and Christianity—all three tell us that we must overcome evil by good. The law of Manu of Hinduism has this to say:

> Let him patiently hear hard words. Let him not insult anybody. Against an angry man let him not in return show anger. Let him bless when he is cursed.

Laws of Manu 6: 47

Buddha in his (teaching) Dhammapada (the path of righteousness) says:

48

Overcome anger by peacefulness. Overcome evil by good; overcome the mean by generosity, and man who lies by truth.

Dhammapada 17: 223

Our Blessed Lord tells us:

You have heard the Commandment, an eye for an eye, a tooth for a tooth, but what I say to you is offer no resistance to injury. When a person strikes you on the right cheek, turn and offer him the other. If anyone wants to go to law over your shirt, hand him over your shirt. Should anyone press you into service for one mile, go with him two miles. Give to the man who begs from you. Do not turn your back on the borrower.

Matthew 5: 38–42

St. Paul in his letter to the Romans speaks thus:

Bless your persecutors; bless and do not curse them. Never repay injury with injury. Beloved, do not avenge yourselves, leave that to God's wrath, for it is written vengeance is mine. I will repay says the Lord. But if your enemy is hungry, feed him, if he is thirsty give him something to drink; by doing this, you will heap burning coals upon his head. Do not be conquered by evil but conquer evil with good.

Romans 12: 14, 17, 19, 20–21

The Supreme example is Christ, who said in the Sermon on the Mount: "Love your enemies, pray for your persecutors."

And he puts this into practice on the Cross: "Father forgive them for they do not know what they do." (Luke 23: 34)

When God's people are oppressed by wicked people, God will come to save them. The similar ideas are expressed in the Bhagavad-Gita of the Hindus and the Bible of the Christians.

49

The Bhagavad-Gita (the Divine Song) says this:

When righteousness declines (O Bharata), when wickedness is strong, I rise from age to age and take visible shape, and move a man with men, succoring the good, thrusting the evil back, and setting Virtue on her seat again.

Bhagavad-Gita 4: 22–27

The Book of Exodus from the Bible has this point to tell us—God from the burning bush called out to Moses and said:

I have witnessed the affliction of my people in Egypt and have heard their cry of complaint against their slave drivers. So I know well what they are suffering. Therefore I have come down to rescue them from the hands of the Egyptians and lead them out of that land. So indeed the cry of the Israelites has reached me, and I have truly noted that the Egyptians are oppressing them. Come, now, I will send you to Pharaoh to lead my people, the Israelites, out of Egypt.

Exodus 3: 7–8, 9–10

Renunciation or self denial is the core and heart of the doctrine of Satyagraha (truth-force). Non-violence renunciation means absence of hankering after fruit.

Bhagavad-Gita says:

Do your duty, but do not worry about the result of your duty. Do not worry about the fruit of your action. Do your duty without expecting a remuneration for it. Do not be attached to the outcome of the duty. The ignorant work for the fruit of their action; The wise must work also without desire pointing man's feet to the path of his duty.

B. G. 3: 50–55

Jesus tells us whatever we do, fasting, praying, almsgiving, or any other thing we do, we must not do with the motive of getting something. We must leave it to the Heavenly Father. (Matthew 6: 1–18)

Buddha says when we do something good we must be like the rock that is not shaken by the wind. So we must not be shaken by fame, name, or blame. (Dhammapada 81)

Love and truth are very essential qualities of non-violence. One must be truthful in thought, word, and deed. These ideas are well expressed by Buddha in his Dhammapada.

He who hurts not with his thoughts or words or deeds, who keeps these three under control—him I call a Brahmin.

Dhammapada 391

The Thirukkural of the Tamils, speaking about truth, has this beautiful statement:

Truth is not only abstaining from killing the person physically but also not killing the person by tongue. What is truth? It is speaking in such a way that may not bring him harm any way.

Kural 291

As our Blessed Lord says in the Sermon on the Mount:

You have heard the Commandment imposed on your forefathers, You shall not commit murder. Every murderer shall be liable to judgment. What I say to you is everyone who grows angry with his brother shall be liable to judgment. Any man who uses abusive language toward his brother shall be answerable to the Sanhedrin.

Matthew 5: 21–22

Love was the fundamental virtue in the ethics of Jesus because love is the society making quality. When Christ said, "You shall love your neighbor as yourself," Jesus treated self-respect as the basis for respect for all persons. A person must have proper self-regard, a reverence for oneself. A person must respect his own integrity and uniqueness. He must love and understand himself. Only then will he be able to love and respect others. We can call Christianity a religion of self-evaluation. That's why Christ gave the loving commandment to the world when He said, "Go, therefore, and make disciples of all nations . . . Teach them to carry out everything I have commanded you." This loving commandment is what Christ gave at the last supper:

> I give you a new Commandment: love one another. Such as my love has been for you, so must your love be for each other. This is how all will know you for my disciples, by your love for one another.
>
> John 13: 34–35

Just like Jesus gave the loving commandment to the world, Buddha gave the ethics of non-violence or compassion to the world. Buddha, in challenging the values of violence, taught that hatreds are not quenched by hatred but by love, and defined a truthfinder as one who lays aside the sword, lives a life of innocence and mercy, heals divisions, and cements friendship . . . for in peace is his delight. Buddha revealed the universal scope of his compassion as he commanded his disciples:

> Go unto all lands and preach this gospel. Tell them that the poor and the lowly, the rich and the high, all are one, and that all castes unite in this religion as do the rivers of the sea.

Conclusion

It is impossible for snakes and wild beasts dominated by their instinct to keep from resisting with all their power, anyone who causes them to suffer. But for us, created in the image of God, guided by reason, to whom it has been given to know God, who have received our law from Him, it is indeed possible for us to love those who hate us. And so when the Lord says: "Love your enemies and do good to those who hate you" (Matthew 5: 44), He is not commanding the impossible but obviously what is possible.

Love and justice are at the center of the non-violent movement. I believe one day justice will roll down like water, and righteousness like a mighty stream.

No lie can live forever. Truth crushed to earth will rise again.

Truth forever on the scaffold,
Wrong forever on the throne.
Yet that scaffold sways the future;
And behind the dim unknown stands God
Within the shadow keeping watch above
His own.

In the words of the late President John F. Kennedy:

Mankind must put an end to war. Or war will put an end to mankind.

The greatest challenge of the day is
how to bring about a revolution of
the heart.
A revolution which has to start
with each one of us.

53

When we begin to take the lowest
place,
to wash the feet of others,
To love our brothers and sisters,
with that burning love,
That passion which led to the Cross,
then we can truly say,
now I have begun.

Dorothy Day,
Loaves and Fishes

The author in the backyard of Bill and Anne
Pelletier's home.

Chapter 7

The Concept of Hospitality According to Bible and Kural

According to the Bible, the virtue of hospitality is a primary virtue of every Christian and every man in this world. Every man will be judged on the Last Judgment Day by this virtue.[1]

Even the early Israelites, when they were in the desert, considered this virtue as the primary virtue of every householder. Hospitality should be extended even to one's enemy once he comes to one's home. Thereby, reconciliation is restored by hospitality.

The act of hospitality is considered holy and the guest is to be regarded as a holy person. The guest at home enjoys all protections from the members of the household, even to the extent of endangering the lives of the family members.

Jesus Christ and the early Christians gave new and deeper meaning to this concept of hospitality. To be hospitable is to remain in Jesus. (Menein) One who is hospitable will be dynamic and will have unceasing and everlasting growth into the very person of Christ. The parable of the Good Samaritan forcefully brings out this idea.[2]

The outpouring of love is hospitality. Hence Thiruvalluvar has placed the chapter on Cherishing Guests after the chapter on The Possession of Love.[3]

Whoever comes to one's home is to be welcomed by cheerful countenance and by kind words. This was considered as the hallmark of Tamil culture. Seeing another man's pain as one's own pain, sympathizing with him in his heart and serving him is considered as real wealth by the Tamil moralists. The Tamils were hospitable even though they were in dire poverty.[4] Hospitality was cherished by the Tamils as the virtue of virtues.[5]

Now let us see how the Biblical sages and Tamil moralist, Thiruvalluvar, agree on the basic need of hospitality for men of all times.

St. Peter in his epistle is admonishing the early Christians "to practice hospitality ungrudgingly to one another." (1 Peter 4: 9) Zacchaeus, the chief tax collector, was a rich man. He was a short man, who wanted to see Jesus but could not because of the crowd. So he ran ahead of the crowd and climbed a sycamore tree to see Jesus, who was going to pass that way. When Jesus came to that place, He looked up and said to Zacchaeus, "Hurry down, Zacchaeus, because I must stay in your house today." Luke goes on to say that Zacchaeus *hurried down and welcomed Him* with great joy. (Luke 19: 1–6)

A very similar idea is expressed in Kural, thus:

With smiling face he entertains each virtuous guest,
"Fortune" with gladsome mind shall in his dwelling rest.

Kural 84

Lakshmi with joyous mind shall dwell in the house of that man who, with *cheerful countenance* entertains the good as guests. And hospitality loses its value when one does not welcome the guest wholeheartedly. This is expressed as in:

The flower of "Anicha" withers away
If you do but its fragrance inhale.
If the face of the host cold welcome convey,

57

The guest's heart within him will fail.

Kural 90

As the Anicham flower fades in smelling, so fades the guest when the face is turned away.

In 1 Kings 17: 9–24 of the Bible, we have a nice and touching incident of hospitality. Elijah is sent to a town of Zarephath, near Sidon. As he came to the town gate, he saw a widow gathering firewood. The prophet is asking for water and bread. The widow said, "By the Living Lord, your God, I swear that I don't have any bread. All I have is a handful of *flour* in a bowl and a bit of olive *oil* in a jar. I came here to gather some firewood to take back home and prepare what little I have for my son and me. That will be our last meal, and then we will starve to death."

"Don't worry," Elijah said to her. "Go and prepare your meal. But first make a small loaf from what you have and bring it to me, and then prepare the rest for you and your son. For this is what the Lord, the God of Israel says, 'The bowl will not run out of flour or the jar run out of oil before the day that I, the Lord, send rain.' "

The widow went and did as Elijah had told her, and all of them had enough food for many days. As the Lord had promised through Elijah, the bowl did not run out of flour nor did the jar run out of oil (1 Kings 17: 9–24). In spite of her utter poverty, the widow performed the act of hospitality whereby she was rewarded: the bowl did not run out of flour and the jar did not run out of oil. She had a surplus. She had more than enough.

Who first regales his guest, and then himself supplies,
O'er all his fields, unsown, shall plenteous harvest rise.

Kural 85

Is it necessary to sow the field of the man who, having provided food for his guests, eats what may remain; when there is sufficient rain, the seeds will sprout in the field and will give enough food to the one who shows hospitality.

In the book of Genesis of the Bible, we find that because Lot gave shelter and protection to guests, he and his household members were protected from harm. (Genesis 19: 1–11)

A parallel thought is expressed by Thiruvalluvar as follows:

Each day he tends the coming guest with kindly care;
Painless, unfailing plenty shall his household share.

Kural 83

The domestic life of the man who daily entertains the guests who come to him shall not be laid waste by poverty.

Abraham at the sacred trees of Mamre was sitting at the entrance of his tent during the hottest part of the day. He looked up and saw three men standing there. As soon as he saw them, he ran out to meet them. Bowing down with his face touching the ground, he said, "Sirs, please do not pass by my home without stopping. I am here to serve you. Let me bring some water for you to wash your feet. I will also bring a bit of food, it will give you strength to continue your journey. You have honored me by coming to my home. So let me serve you." They replied, "Thank you, we accept."

Abraham hurried into the tent and said to Sarah, "Quick, take a sack of your best flour and bake some bread." Then he ran to the herd and picked out a calf that was tender and fat, and gave it to a servant, who hurried to get it ready. He took some cream, some milk and the meat, and set the food before the men. There, under the tree, he served them himself and they ate (Genesis 18: 1–8). Yes, the three men who came to Abraham were not mere human beings, they were angels of

God. Just because Abraham performed the act of hospitality, he and his wife were blessed by God with a child in their old age.

Again, St. Paul says to the Hebrews, "Remember to welcome strangers in your homes. There were some who did that and welcomed angels without knowing it." (Hebrews 13: 2)

Thiruvalluvar gives the same idea in a nutshell in the following couplet:

The guest arrived, he tends; the coming guest expects to see;
To those in Heavenly homes that dwell a welcome guest is
    he.

Kural 86

He who, having entertained the guests that have come, looks not for others who may yet come, will be a welcomed guest to the inhabitants of Heaven.

Hospitality done to the poor is hospitality rendered to Christ. "I tell you, whenever you did this for one of the least important of these brothers of Mine, you did it for Me" (Matthew 25: 40). This is the best way of stocking reward in the next world. "Do not store up riches for yourselves here on earth, where moths and rust destroy and robbers break in and steal. Instead store up riches where moths and rust cannot destroy and robbers break in and steal" (Matthew 6: 19–20).

Thiruvalluvar has the same note in his Kural when he says:

With pain they guard their stores,
Yet "all forlorn are we," they'll cry,
Who cherish not their guests,
Nor kindly help supply.

Kural 88

Those who have taken no part in the benevolence of hospitality shall (at length lament), saying, "We have labored and laid up wealth, and are now without support."

Synthesis

1. Both the Bible and the Kural advocate the practice of hospitality unceasingly and ungrudgingly.
2. These two sacred books agree that hospitality will procure rewards in this world as well as in the next.
3. By cherishing the guests, one is entertaining the Heavenly guests—these are the parallel thoughts of these two sacred books.
4. Hospitality is a passport to Heaven.
5. In the Bible, Christ says "that those who have not rendered hospitality to the *poor* (who represent Him in this world) will have eternal punishment." The King will reply, "I tell you, whenever you refused to help one of these least important ones, you refused to help Me." These, then, will be sent off to eternal punishment, but the righteous (one who does hospitality) will go to eternal life (Matthew 25: 45-46).

Thiruvalluvar, too, says that those who have treasured and stored up riches and wealth without doing hospitality will cry and lament at the end of their life.

Notes

1. Matthew 25: 44–45
2. Luke 10: 25–37. John 1: 39; 3: 21; 5: 40; 6: 35; 6: 37; 7: 37.
3. 8—The Possession of Love; 9—Cherishing Guests.
4. Puram 333, 316; Kural 43.
5. Manimekalai Kathai 25, lines 228–231;
Manimekalai Kathai 13, lines 109–115.
6. English version of Kural is taken from Dr. G. U. Pope.
7. Bible—Good News Bible (TEV)—Today's English Version.
8. *Dictionary of the Bible*—McKenzie, S.J.